DISCOVER
JOSHUA 1–8

I Will Be with You

STUDY GUIDE

We thank Meg Garber of Burke, Virginia, for writing this study.

Unless otherwise noted, Scripture quotations in this publication are from the HOLY BIBLE, NEW INTERNATIONAL VERSION, © 1973, 1978, 1984, International Bible Society. Used by permission of Zondervan Bible Publishers.

Discover Your Bible series. *Discover Joshua—Conquering the Land,* © 2000, Faith Alive Christian Resources, 1700 28th St. SE, Grand Rapids, MI 49508-1407. All rights reserved. Printed in the United States of America.

We welcome your comments. Call us at 1-800-272-5125 or e-mail us at info@DiscoverYourBible.org.

ISBN 978-1-56212-577-6

10 9 8 7 6 5 4 3

Contents

How to Study 4

Introduction. 5

Glossary of Terms 6

Lesson 1
   Take Possession of the Land 8

Lesson 2
   From Fear to Faith 11

Lesson 3
   "Deep River" 14

Lesson 4
   Remembering God. 16

Lesson 5
   Conquering Jericho 18

Lesson 6
   Sudden Defeat 21

Lesson 7
   Victory at Ai 24

Evaluation

How to Study

The questions in this study booklet will help you discover for yourself what the Bible says. This is inductive Bible study—no one will tell you what the Bible says or what to believe. You will discover the message for yourself.

Questions are the key to inductive Bible study. Through questions you will search for the writers' thoughts and ideas. The prepared questions in this booklet are designed to help you in your quest for answers. You can and should ask your own questions too. The Bible comes alive with meaning for many people as they discover for themselves the exciting truths it contains. Our hope and prayer is that this booklet will help the Bible come alive for you.

The questions are designed to be used with the New International Version of the Bible, but other translations can also be used.

Step 1. Read the Bible passage several times. Allow the thoughts and ideas to sink in. Think about its meaning. Ask questions of your own about the passage.

Step 2. Answer the questions, drawing your answers from the passage. Remember that the purpose of the study is to discover what the Bible says. Write your answers in your own words. If you use Bible study aids such as commentaries or Bible handbooks, do so only after completing your own personal study.

Step 3. Apply the Bible's message to your own life and world. Ask yourself these questions: What is this passage saying to me? How does it challenge me? Comfort me? Encourage me? Is there a promise I should claim? A warning I should heed? For what can I give thanks? If you sense God speaking to you in some way, respond in a personal prayer.

Step 4. Share your thoughts with someone else if possible. This will be easiest if you are part of a Bible study group that meets regularly to share discoveries and discuss questions.

Introduction

You are in for an adventure. The book of Joshua is both inspiring and combative. In this book God's people, the Israelites, do what they had refused to do when Moses was their leader—enter and occupy the promised land. But this isn't just imaginative adventure and inspiration; it is true history. It is history rich with meaning for all of us. This study will lead you to ask if Joshua's God is not the same God you know of. Through this study you will come to know him more fully. As Lucy from *The Chronicles of Narnia* says of Aslan, "He is not a tame lion." Neither is our God tame. But he is completely good, just, loving, wise, and merciful. In the story of Joshua and the Israelites you will see Jesus and you will see yourself.

The overall purpose of the study is to see how God works out the redemption of his people from slavery in Egypt by fulfilling his promise to settle Abraham's descendants in a new and fertile homeland. Through Joshua, the man who led the Israelites into the promised land after Moses' death, God kept his promise and gave salvation to his people. But not only is this a history of people who lived long ago and far away, it is the history of everyone who is God's child. For from beginning to end the Bible is a record and revelation of how God saves people and brings them into a spiritual homeland.

Your group members might ask, "What is the relevance of a book of ancient biblical history?" The answer is that the book of Joshua is highly relevant for people today. As we investigate the book together we will find

- a history of the Israelites and their leader. Moses led the Israelites out of Egypt, but they would not trust God to give them the promised land. When Moses died, Joshua led them successfully into the promised land.
- a foreshadowing of God's salvation of people after Joshua's time.
- a word from God about our own lives, just as God spoke into Joshua's situation and life.

May God bless your study of his Word.

Meg Garber
Burke, Virginia

Glossary of Terms

Achan—a man of the tribe of Judah who violated the ban on plunder from Jericho by stealing valuable items.

Ai—a Canaanite city east of Bethel that Israel conquered after the defeat of Jericho.

ark of the covenant—a sacred, rectangular box made of acacia wood and covered with gold, symbolizing God's presence among his people.

burnt offering—a sacrifice to God for sins involving the burning of a whole animal. The worshiper placed his hands on the animal to show that it was a sacrifice for his own sins. The sacrificial animal could have no imperfection.

Canaanites—inhabitants of the land of Canaan.

circumcision—cutting off the foreskin of the penis. Circumcision symbolized the cutting away of sin from one's life. Abraham's descendants were required to do this to show that they belonged to God's chosen people.

conquest—conquering and/or acquiring territory.

consecrate—to make, declare, or set apart as holy.

covenant—a binding agreement made by two or more persons or parties; a compact; a contract.

Deuteronomy—the fifth book of the Old Testament, in which the Law of Moses is stated for the second time.

devoted—dedicated or consecrated.

fellowship offering—similar to the burnt offering, except that only the fat (considered by the Israelites to be the best portion) was burned on the altar, and the meat was shared by the worshiper and his family. Because God also shared in the sacrifice, it was thought of as a friendship meal with God.

Israelites—descendants of Abraham, Isaac, and Jacob (whom God renamed Israel). God chose the Israelites to be his people (Ex. 3:9-10).

Jericho—an ancient city situated at 800 feet below sea level near the northern end of the Dead Sea; captured by the Israelites in the thirteenth century B.C.

Joshua—leader of the Israelites after Moses' death. His name means "the LORD saves." The Hebrew name *Joshua* is the same as the Greek name *Jesus*.

manna—the food miraculously provided for the Israelites in the wilderness after their escape from Egypt.

Moses—the great prophet who led the Israelites from slavery in Egypt through the desert to the border of Canaan. He received from God and taught to Israel the laws that would govern them as God's chosen people.

Passover—a Jewish festival that commemorates the Israelites' escape from Egypt.

promised land—the land of Canaan, promised to Abraham and his descendants.

Rahab—a prostitute who lived in a house on the wall of Jericho. She hid Joshua's two spies because she believed God would give Canaan to the Israelites.

reproach—shame or disgrace.

Reubenites, Gadites, and half-tribe of Manasseh—some of the tribes of the Israelite people.

sovereign—paramount; supreme; self-governing; independent.

Lesson 1
Joshua 1:1-18

Take Possession of the Land

1. *Joshua 1:1-5*
   a. What milestone are the Israelites experiencing as the book of Joshua opens?

   b. Read Deuteronomy 1:19-46. Summarize the events in this passage as a background to Joshua.

   c. What promises does God make in these verses?

2. *Joshua 1:6-9*
   a. Why is Joshua to be strong and courageous (v. 6)?

   b. What lifestyle results in prosperity and success? Why is this message repeated twice?

   c. On what basis does God command Joshua to put terror and discouragement aside?

3. *Joshua 1:10-11*
   a. What are the officers to tell the people to do?

   b. What guarantee will the people have?

4. *Joshua 1:12-15*
   a. What does Joshua tell the Reubenites, Gadites, and the half-tribe of Manasseh?

   b. Put into your own words God's command to these three tribes.

   c. How do the Israelites know this land is for them? How many times in this chapter has that been repeated?

5. *Joshua 1:16-18*
   a. How do the Israelites respond to God's instructions? How is this response emphasized?

   b. What is the consequence of disobedience?

6. *Joshua 1:1-18*
   a. List several of the dominant themes that are repeated in this chapter.

   b. Considering those themes, what title would you give this chapter? Why?

Lesson 2
Joshua 2:1-24

From Fear to Faith

1. *Joshua 2:1-7*
   a. Considering Joshua's trust in God as expressed in chapter 1, why do you think Joshua sends spies to Jericho?

   b. If you were to give a title to this section, what would it be? Why?

   c. Who are the three characters (or character groups) of this passage? What is the "special interest" of each one, and how do they act in accordance with that interest?

   d. Do you think Rahab is right or wrong to tell a lie in this situation? Why?

2. *Joshua 2:8-11*
   a. What does Rahab confess to the spies?

b. How does Rahab arrive at this belief?

   c. How would you describe Rahab's response to the Israelites' God? Why might she have responded in this way?

3. *Joshua 2:12-21*
   a. What are the terms of the agreement between Rahab and the Israelite spies?

   b. On what basis does Rahab ask for deliverance from destruction?

   c. What symbol does Rahab exhibit to show that the agreement remains binding?

   d. Does it appear that Rahab can be trusted? Why or why not?

4. *Joshua 2:22-24*
   a. What does the spies' diligence in following Rahab's advice tell us about her character?

b. What do the spies conclude in their report to Joshua?

5. **Joshua 2:1-24**

   a. Throughout this chapter, phrases such as "melting in fear" and "hearts sank and . . . courage failed" contrast sharply with the frequently repeated theme of chapter 1, "be strong and courageous." What do you think is being contrasted between chapters 1 and 2? Why?

   b. To which do you more closely relate—courage or fear? Why?

   c. Think about a time in your life that evoked either courage or fear. How do chapters 1 and 2 of Joshua help you understand your feelings in that situation?

Lesson 3
Joshua 3:1-4:24

"Deep River"

1. *Joshua 3:1-6*

   a. What and whom are the Israelites to follow when they move on from the banks of the Jordan?

   b. Look up the word "consecrate" in the glossary. What does it mean? Why do you think the Lord wants the people to consecrate themselves?

2. *Joshua 3:7-17*

   a. What is evidently necessary in order for Joshua to lead effectively in Israel?

   b. How many times is the ark of the covenant mentioned in verses 1-17? What role does the ark play in this chapter?

   c. Why does God stop the flow of the Jordan River?

3. *Joshua 4:1-9*
   a. Describe the job of the twelve men Joshua chooses.

   b. What is the purpose of the twelve stones?

4. *Joshua 4:10-18*
   a. Who leads the Israelites in crossing the Jordan? Why?

   b. On what does the Israelites' safety in crossing the Jordan River depend?

   c. How is Joshua's being exalted by the Lord different than his being exalted through the exercise of his own leadership?

5. *Joshua 3:1-4:18*
   The ark of the covenant is mentioned fourteen times in this passage. Glance over verses 3:3, 4, 6, 8, 11, 13, 14, and 17; and 4:5, 7, 9, 11, 16, and 18. What seems to be the role of the ark of the covenant among the Israelites?

Lesson 4
Joshua 4:19-5:12

Remembering God

1. *Joshua 4:19-5:1*
   a. What is the purpose of the pile of twelve stones?

   b. Should the Israelites be proud of their accomplishment in crossing the Jordan? Why or why not?

   c. What does God say was the purpose of the Israelites' crossing the Jordan? (v. 24)

2. *Joshua 5:2-9*
   a. Look up *circumcision* in the glossary or a dictionary. What is circumcision? What does it symbolize? (See Genesis 17:1-14.)

   b. Why has this particular generation of Israelites never been circumcised?

3. **Joshua 5:10-12**
   a. What feast do the Israelites celebrate?

   b. Of what event does Passover remind the people (see Exodus 12:24-30)?

   c. What do the people eat on the day after the Passover celebration?

   d. Why do you think God stops providing manna? Of what is he reminding the people?

4. **Joshua 4:19-5:12**
   a. What are the three memorials mentioned in this passage?

   b. What kinds of symbols or memorials do believers in Christ use to express, remember, and affirm our faith?

Lesson 5
Joshua 5:13-6:27

Conquering Jericho

1. *Joshua 5:13-6:5*

    a. Whom does Joshua meet outside Jericho? Who might this person actually be?

    b. What does this encounter say about Joshua's character?

    c. What sequence of events leads to the capture of Jericho?

2. *Joshua 6:6-14*

    a. What is the role of the ark of the covenant in the conquest of Jericho?

    b. What is the marching order for the Israelites?

    c. Imagine the scene of the six days described here. What might the people of Jericho be feeling? The Israelites?

3. ***Joshua 6:15-21***
   a. What is different about the seventh day of the conquest?

   b. What two important reminders does Joshua give the Israelites concerning Jericho?

   c. How are the Israelites to treat "devoted" things? What are the consequences for violating this?

4. ***Joshua 6:22-25***
   a. In what way does Rahab experience the blessings of faith in God?

   b. What do the Israelites do to the city after Rahab and her family are rescued?

5. ***Joshua 6:26-27***
   a. What are to be the consequences for anyone who tries to rebuild Jericho? (See 1 Kings 16:34 to find out what happened.)

   b. Why might Joshua have delivered this curse?

c. Why did Joshua, and not God, receive all the credit for the defeat of Jericho?

6. **Joshua 5:13-6:27**
   a. From your study of this passage, use one or two words to describe
      1) the commander of the Lord's army

      2) Joshua

      3) the Israelites

      4) Rahab

   b. Whose battle is this—God's or the Israelites'? Why?

   c. What personal "Jericho" needs to be completely defeated in your life? What do you think is God's battle plan? What might God ask you to do to bring about victory?

Lesson 6
Joshua 7:1-26
Sudden Defeat

1. *Joshua 7:1-5*

   a. What does verse 1 tell us happened during the conquest of Jericho? Why was this wrong to do?

   b. Summarize the events of verses 2-5.

   c. Why were the Israelite soldiers routed by the men of Ai?

2. *Joshua 7:6-9*

   a. Why does Joshua tear his clothes and fall facedown before the ark of the Lord?

   b. What are Joshua's two concerns about the defeat at Ai (v. 9)?

3. *Joshua 7:10-15*

   a. What reason does the Lord give for the Israelites' defeat?

b. What does the Lord require of the Israelites (v. 12)?

c. What course of action does the Lord direct the Israelites to take?

d. Summarize the content of these verses in a cause/effect statement—for example, she ate spoiled food (cause); therefore she got sick (effect).

4. *Joshua 7:16-23*
   a. How was the offender identified?

   b. How would you describe Joshua's words to Achan?

   c. How would you characterize Achan's confession? Shallow? Sincere? Repentant?

   d. How is Achan's confession confirmed?

5. *Joshua 7:24-26*
   a. Do you think Achan knew he was bringing trouble on Israel when he stole the items from Jericho? How do you know?

   b. Summarize the content of these verses in a cause/effect statement.

6. *Joshua 7:1-26*
   a. Why is Achan's disobedience especially serious? (See 7:15.)

   b. Why did the individual sin of one man threaten a whole community of people?

   c. Can you think of an example of personal wrongdoing today that would carry serious consequences for a community of people?

Lesson 7
Joshua 8:1-35

Victory at Ai

1. *Joshua 8:1-8*
   a. Why does Joshua need the Lord's reassurance in 8:1?

   b. What does the Lord tell Joshua for his encouragement?

   c. What is the key to the Lord's plan for the capture of Ai?

   d. Use the space below to draw the military plan Joshua lays out in verses 3-8. Label the key parts of your drawing.

2. *Joshua 8:9-17*

   a. Why is one part of the army to go out the day before and Joshua's force to wait until the next morning?

   b. In what ways are the people of Ai tricked by this military strategy?

   c. What is the key to the success of the ambush?

3. *Joshua 8:18-29*

   a. What signal does Joshua give for ambush? How is the ambush accomplished?

   b. What strategy does Joshua use to defeat the Ai army?

   c. What is Joshua's role in this battle (vv. 18-19, 26)?

   d. Summarize the events that mark the end of Ai.

4. *Joshua 8:30-35*
   a. Read Deuteronomy 11:22-32. How does Joshua 8:30-35 fulfill the Deuteronomy passage?

   b. Picture (you may even want to sketch) the whole nation of Israel as described in verse 33. What role did the ark of the covenant play in this gathering between Ebal and Gerizim?

   c. Verses 30-35 describe the Israelites' worshipful response to the victories over Jericho and Ai. What does the nation of Israel do in their worship?

5. *Joshua 8:1-35*
   a. What does the defeat of Ai teach about the character of God? About the importance of obeying him?

   b. Who listened as Joshua read the entire law that Moses had written? Why do you think this is noted, and what may be the significance for us?

Evaluation

discover Joshua 1-8

Please complete this evaluation. Your input is important. Send the evaluation to Attn. Discover Your Bible, Raise Up Global Ministries, 1700 28th Street SE, Grand Rapids, MI 49508-1407. Or. email your evaluation answers to info@discoveryourbible.org. Thank you.

1. Was this a home group ___ or a church-based ___ program?

2. Was the study used for

    ___ a community evangelism group?

    ___ a community faith-nurture group?

    ___ a church Bible study group?

3. How would you rate the materials?

    Study Guide: ☐ excellent ☐ very good ☐ good ☐ fair ☐ poor

    Leader Guide: ☐ excellent ☐ very good ☐ good ☐ fair ☐ poor

4. What were the strengths and weaknesses of the study?

5. What would you suggest to improve the material?

6. In general, what was the experience of your group?

7. Other comments

Your name (optional) _____

Address _____

DISCOVER YOUR BIBLE

**Thematic:
POWER OF
FORGIVENESS**

To explore similar studies, visit

GlobalCoffeeBreak.org

You can find samples and explore our Old and New Testament and thematic studies in English, Spanish, and Korean.

We are glad you enjoyed this study!

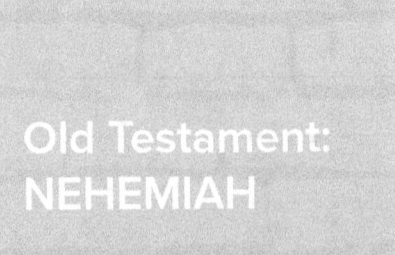

**Old Testament:
NEHEMIAH**

**New Testament:
HEBREWS**

DISCOVER YOUR BIBLE

A Global Coffee Break group is:

- Designed for dynamic group discussions
- Perfect for outreach
- Focused on the biblical text
- Geared for life change

Learn more about Global Coffee Break

GlobalCoffeeBreak.org

www.ingramcontent.com/pod-product-compliance
Lightning Source LLC
Chambersburg PA
CBHW050048080526
44586CB00014B/1509